Exploring Earth's Surface

Printed in Mexico

ISBN-13: 978-0-15-362012-6
ISBN-10: 0-15-362012-9

9 10 0908 16 15 14 13 12 11
4500330474

Harcourt
SCHOOL PUBLISHERS

Weathering

Weathering changes Earth's crust.
Wind and water break down rock.
Weathering can change the shape of rock.

▲ **weathered rock**

Weathering can break rock into small pieces.
Water may freeze in the cracks of a rock.
Ice takes up more space than water.
The ice makes the cracks bigger.
After a while, the rock breaks into pieces.

Erosion

Wind or water may cause erosion.
Wind can move sand or small rocks.
Moving water can move sand or rock.
Erosion changes the shape of land forms.

Earthquakes

▲ **break in land caused by an earthquake**

Earthquakes shake Earth's surface.
They change the surface quickly.
Earthquakes may cause land to rise and fall.
They may cause lakes to form.

Volcanoes

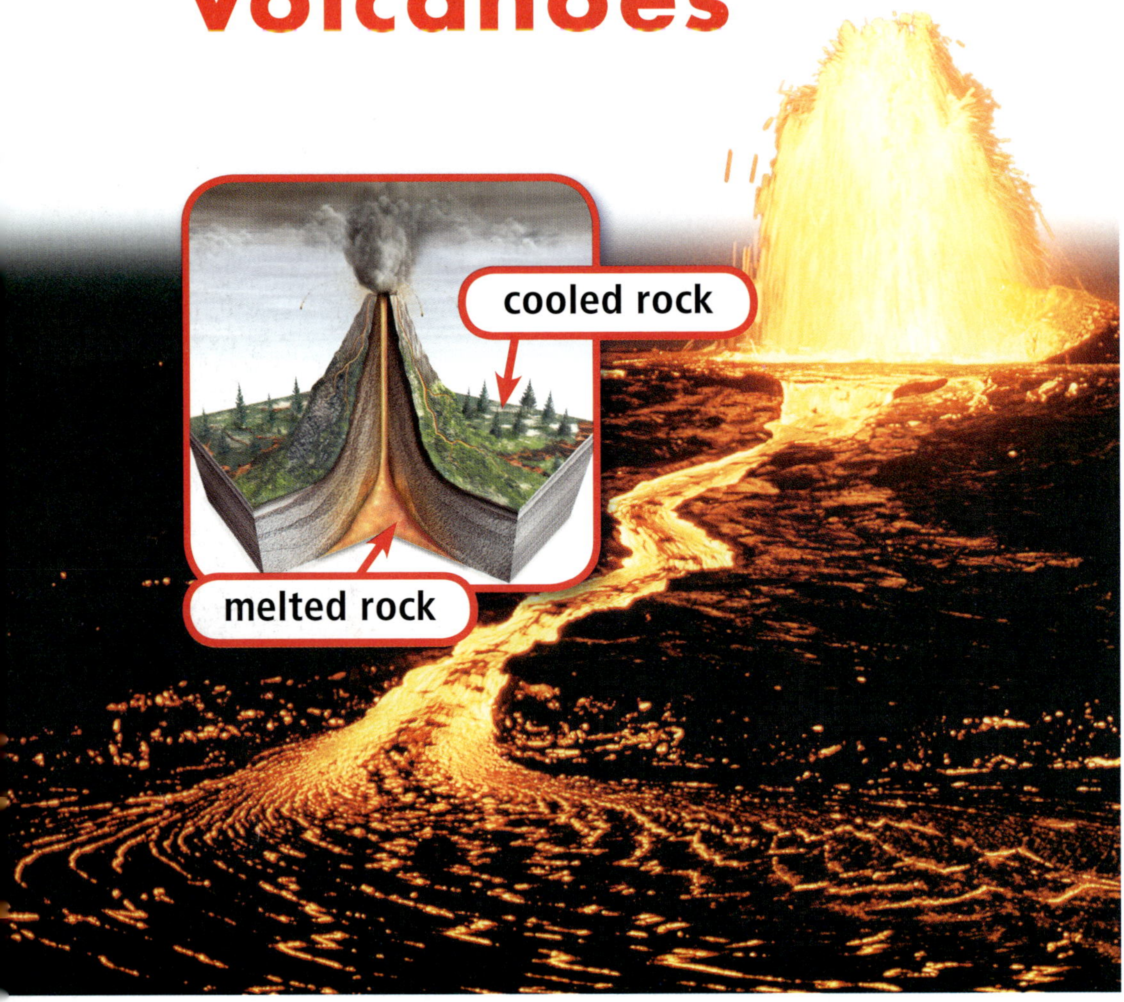

Volcanoes change Earth's surface quickly.
A volcano is a hole in Earth's surface.
Hot, melted rock may flow from the volcano.
As the rock cools, a mountain forms.

Rocks

Rocks are pieces of Earth's crust.
Grains of sand are tiny rocks you can hold.
Boulders are rocks big enough to climb.

limestone

marble

slate

sandstone

granite

obsidian

Rocks are made up of different minerals. That is why they look and feel different. Some rocks are harder than others. Some are smooth. Some are rough.

Soil

Soil is made of bits of rock and other matter.
Most soils have parts of dead plants in them.
There are many kinds of soil.
Different soils look and feel different.

Fossils

model of stegosaurus

fossil of stegosaurus

Dinosaurs lived millions of years ago.
Today they are extinct, or gone.
Fossils show what dinosaurs looked like.
Fossils show extinct plants and animals.

How Fossils Form

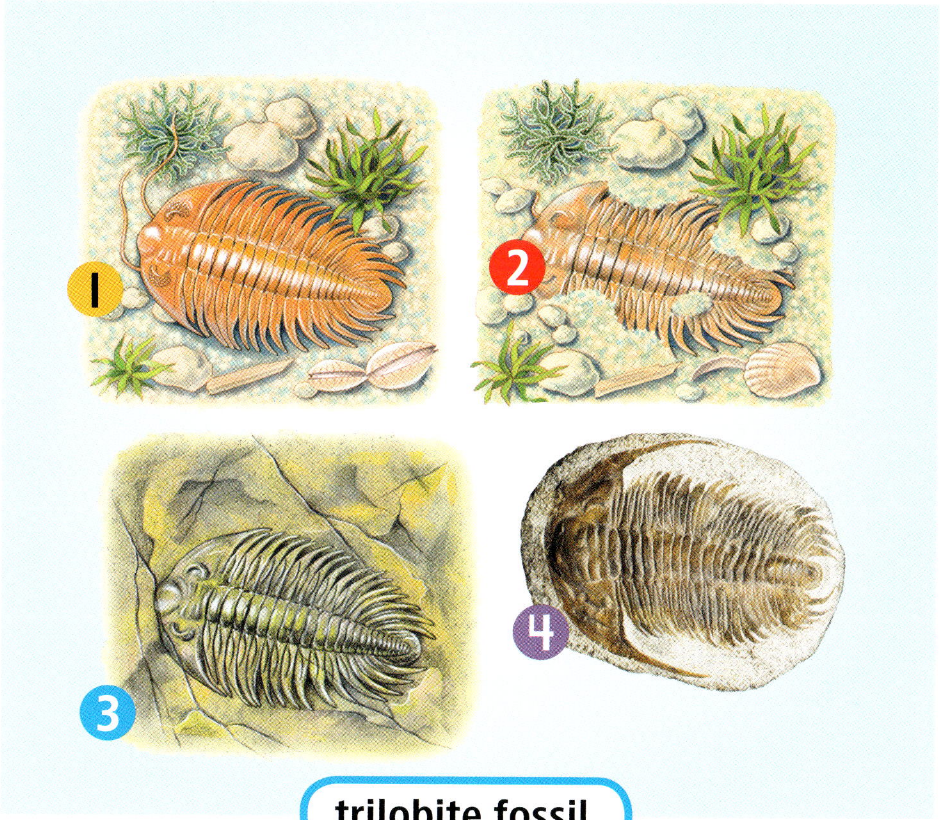

trilobite fossil

1. A plant or animal is buried.
2. The soft parts rot away.
3. The hard parts turn to rock.
4. After millions of years, a fossil is formed.

Vocabulary